Go the Fuck to Sleep

by Adam Mansbach

illustrated by Ricardo Cortés

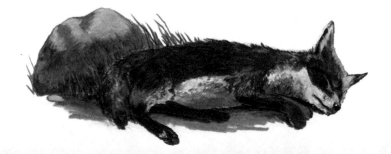

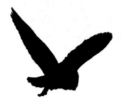

Published by Akashic Books
Words ©2011 Adam Mansbach
Illustrations ©2011 Ricardo Cortés

ISBN-13: 978-1-61775-025-0
Tenth printing

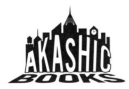

Akashic Books
PO Box 1456
New York, NY 10009
info@akashicbooks.com
www.akashicbooks.com

Adam Mansbach's novels include *The End of the Jews*, winner of the California Book Award, and the best-selling *Angry Black White Boy*, a *San Francisco Chronicle* Best Book of 2005. His fiction and essays have appeared in the *New York Times Book Review*, *The Believer*, *Poets & Writers*, the *Los Angeles Times,* and many other publications. He is the 2011 New Voices Professor of Fiction at Rutgers University. His daughter, Vivien, is three.

www.AdamMansbach.com

Ricardo Cortés has illustrated books about marijuana, electricity, the Jamaican bobsled team, and Chinese food. His work has been featured in the *New York Times, Entertainment Weekly*, the *Village Voice*, the *San Francisco Chronicle,* and on CNN and FOX News. He lives in Brooklyn, where he is working on a book about the history of coffee, cocaine, and Coca-Cola.

www.Rmcortes.com

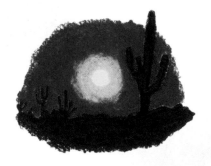

for Vivien, without whom none of this would be possible

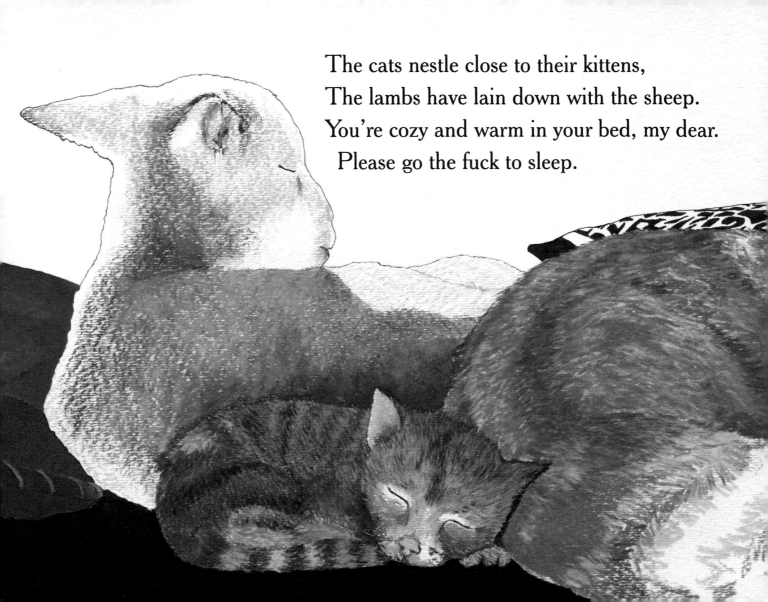

The cats nestle close to their kittens,
The lambs have lain down with the sheep.
You're cozy and warm in your bed, my dear.
Please go the fuck to sleep.

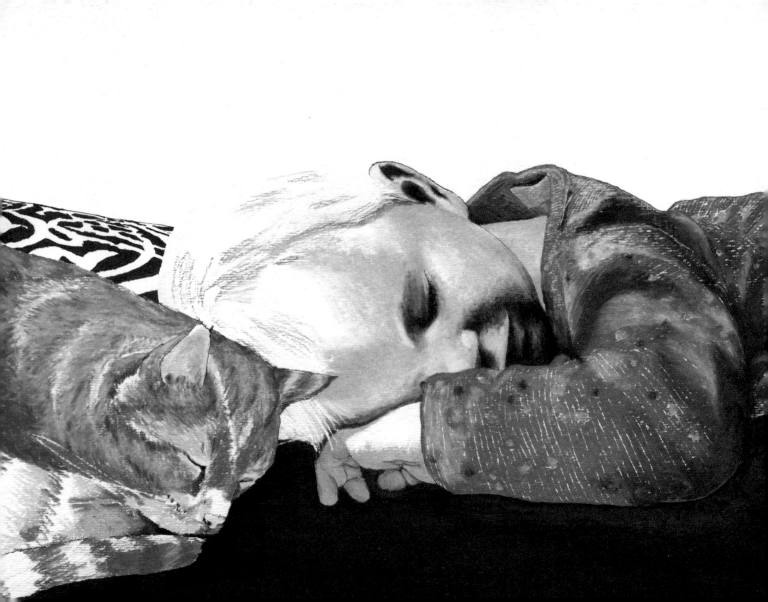

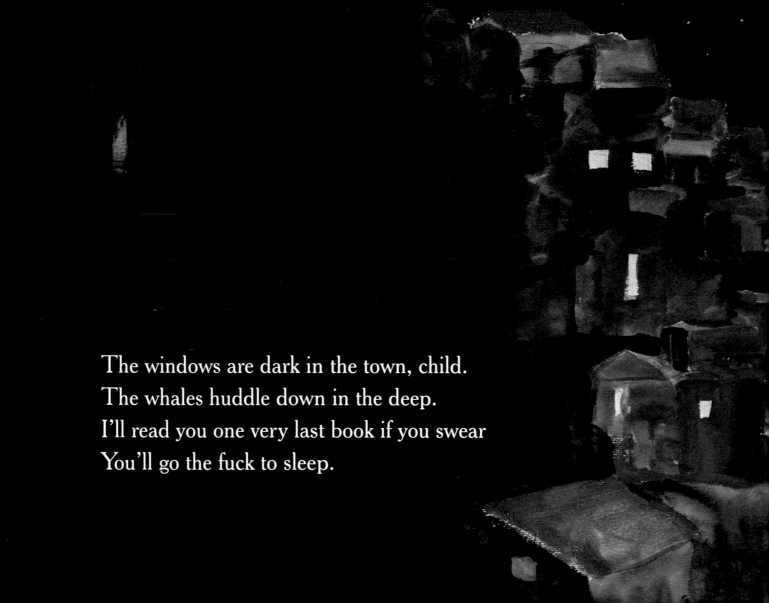

The windows are dark in the town, child.
The whales huddle down in the deep.
I'll read you one very last book if you swear
You'll go the fuck to sleep.

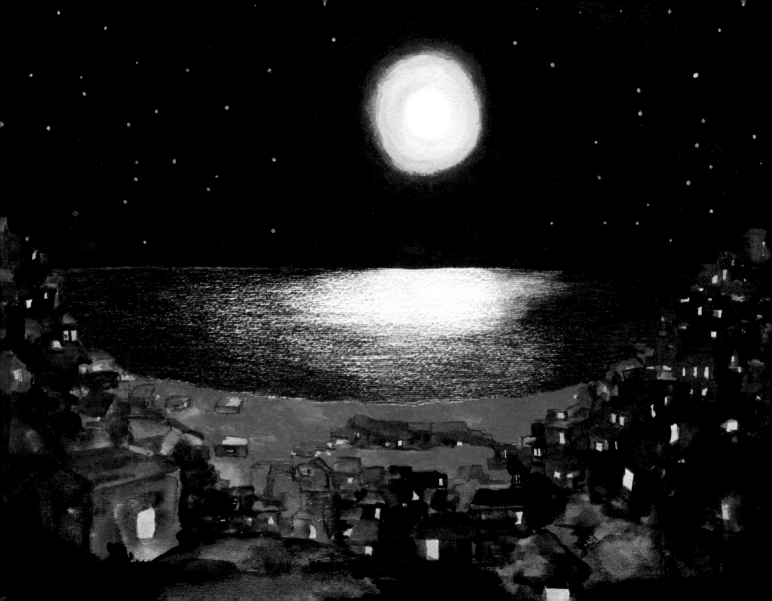

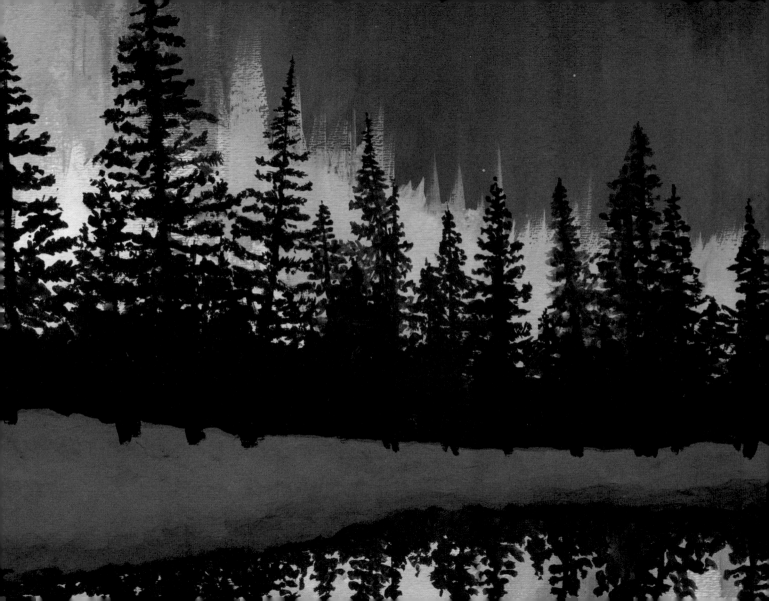

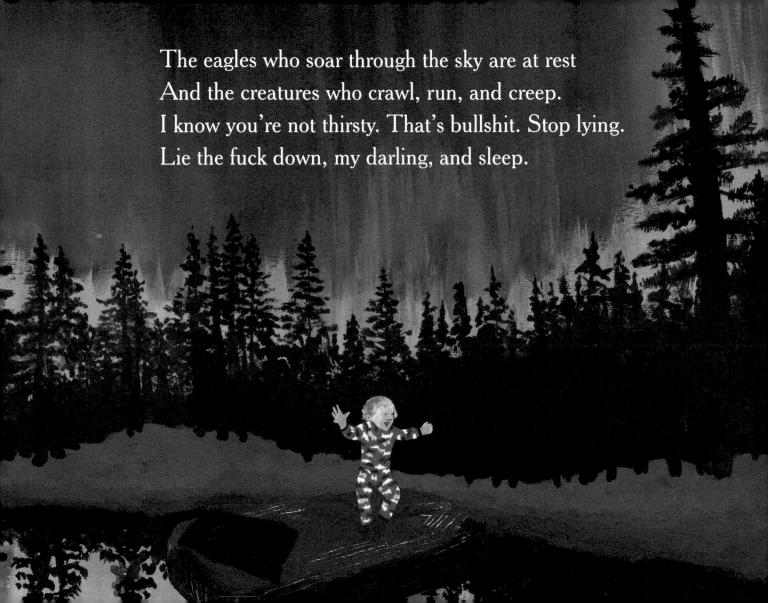

The eagles who soar through the sky are at rest
And the creatures who crawl, run, and creep.
I know you're not thirsty. That's bullshit. Stop lying.
Lie the fuck down, my darling, and sleep.

The wind whispers soft through the grass, hon.
The field mice, they make not a peep.
It's been thirty-eight minutes already.
Jesus Christ, what the fuck? Go to sleep.

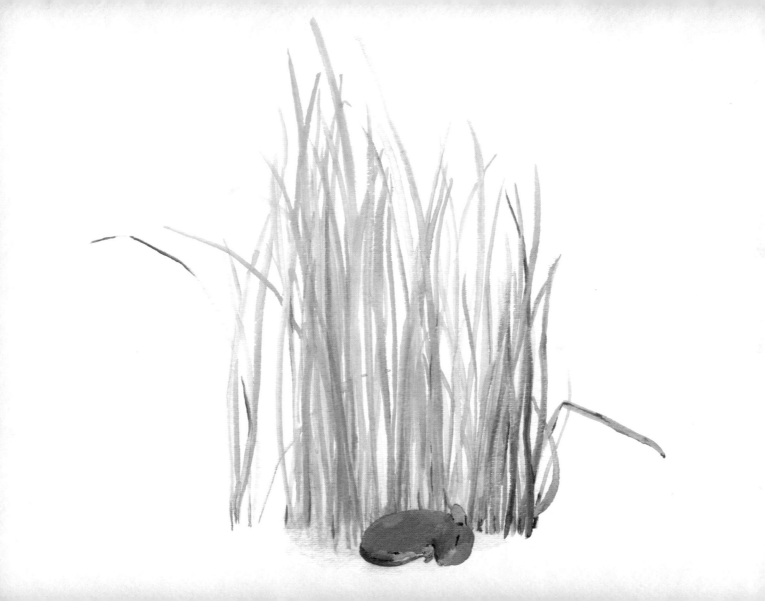

All the kids from day care are in dreamland.
The froggie has made his last leap.
Hell no, you can't go to the bathroom.
You know where you can go? The fuck to sleep.

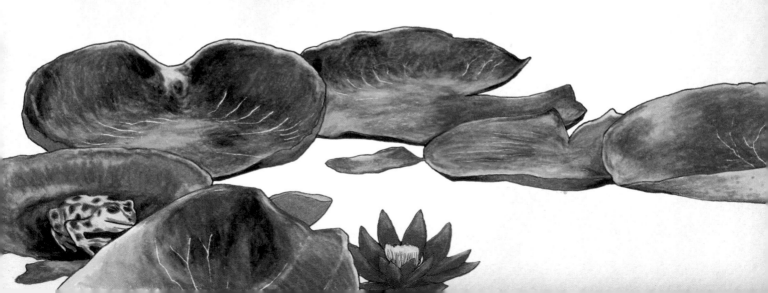

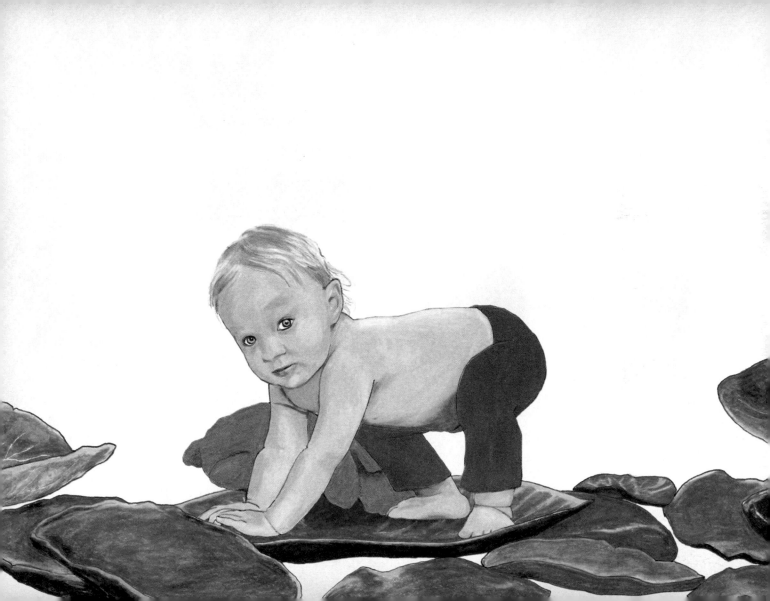

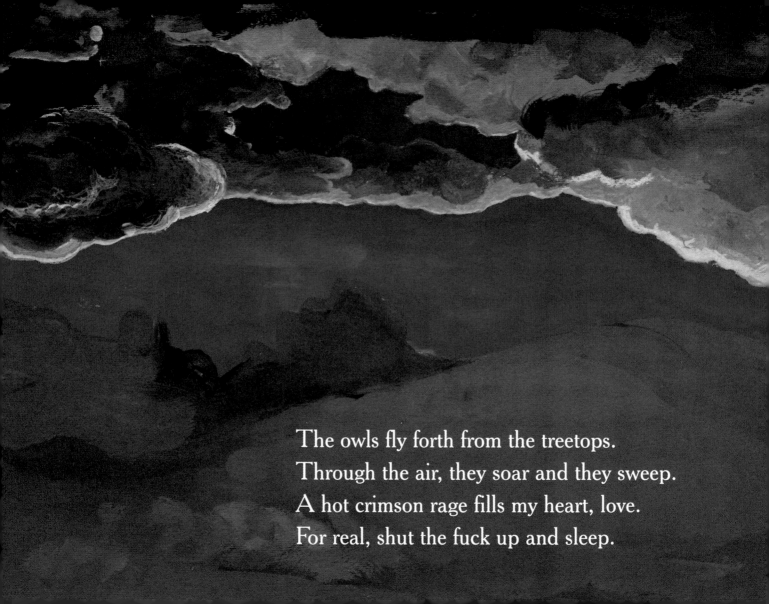

The owls fly forth from the treetops.
Through the air, they soar and they sweep.
A hot crimson rage fills my heart, love.
For real, shut the fuck up and sleep.

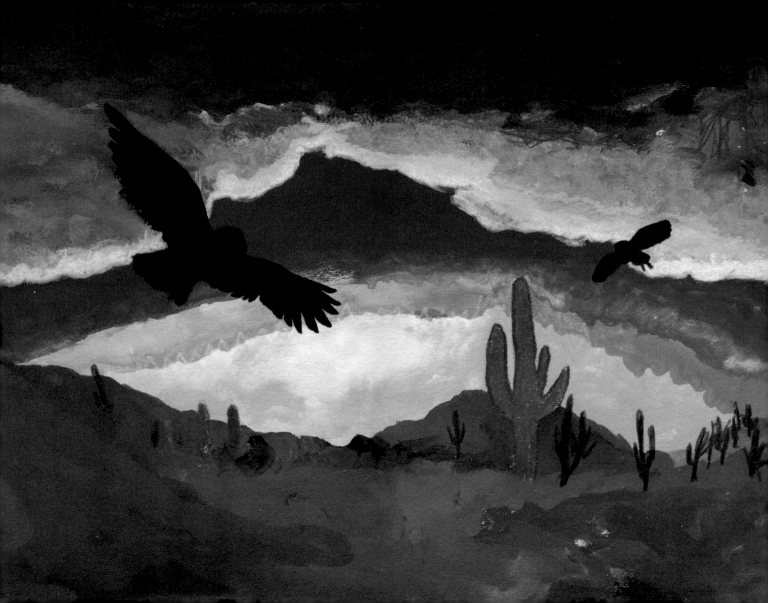

The cubs and the lions are snoring,
Wrapped in a big snuggly heap.
How come you can do all this other great shit
But you can't lie the fuck down and sleep?

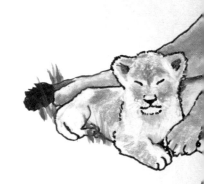

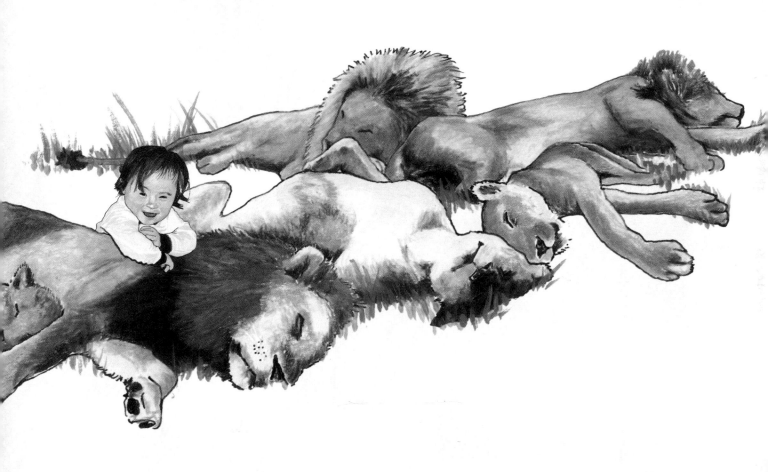

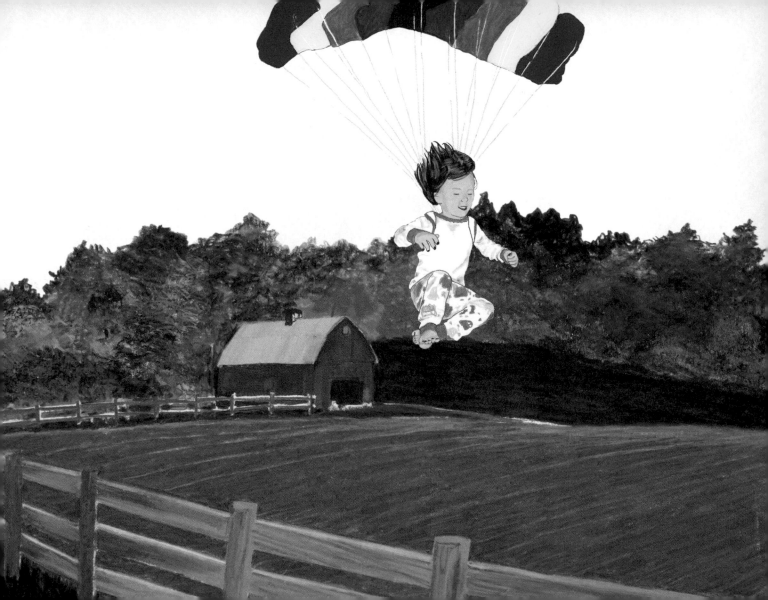

The seeds slumber beneath the earth now
And the crops that the farmers will reap.
No more questions. This interview's over.
I've got two words for you, kid: fucking sleep.

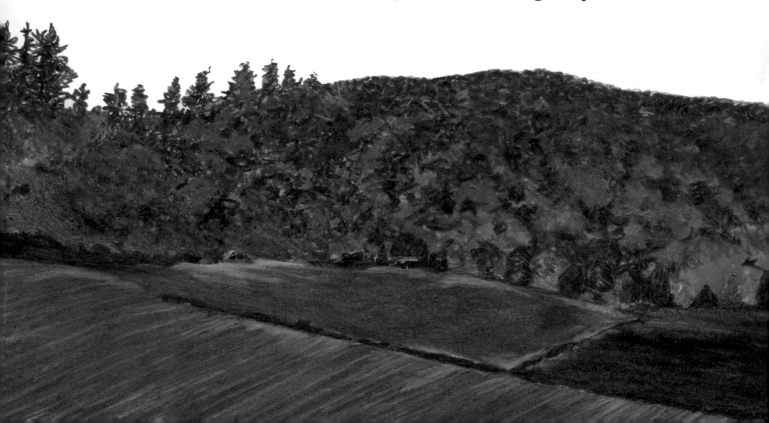

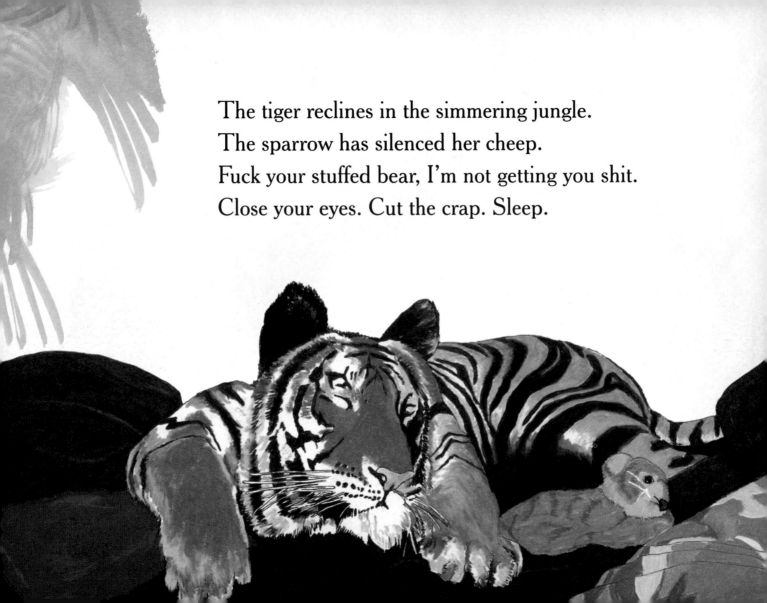

The tiger reclines in the simmering jungle.
The sparrow has silenced her cheep.
Fuck your stuffed bear, I'm not getting you shit.
Close your eyes. Cut the crap. Sleep.

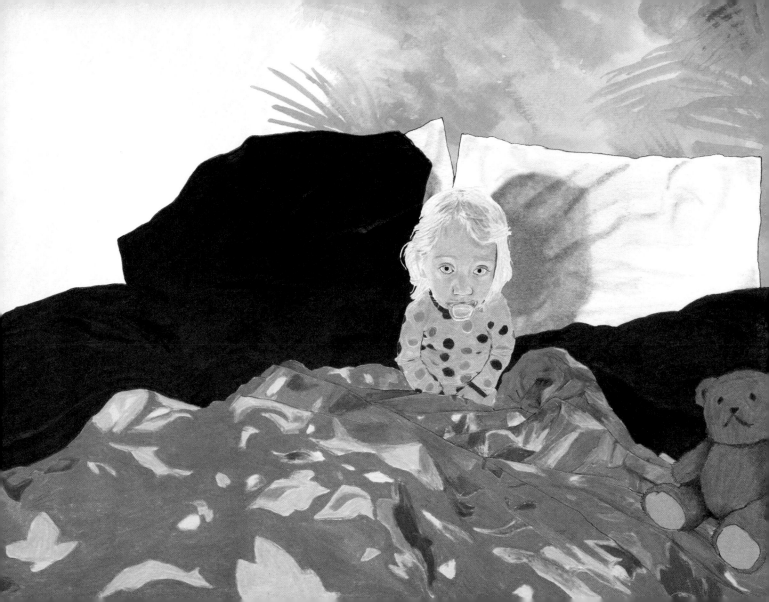

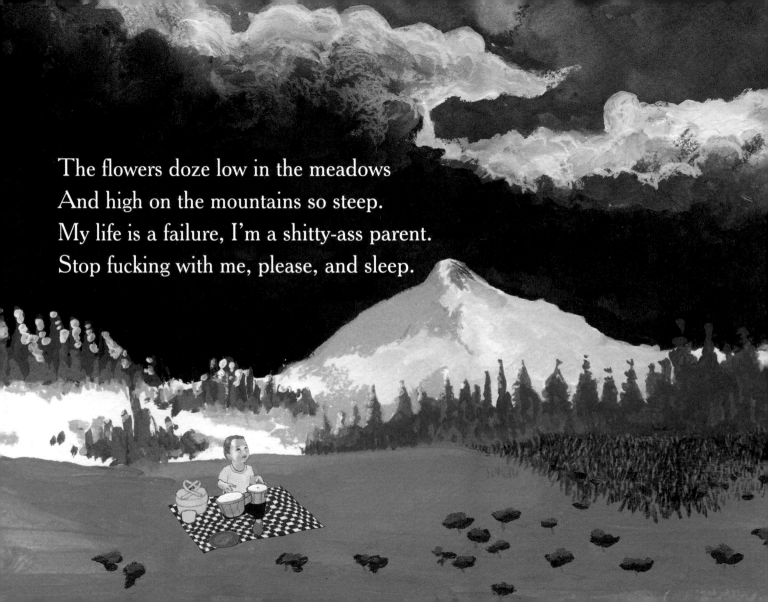

The flowers doze low in the meadows
And high on the mountains so steep.
My life is a failure, I'm a shitty-ass parent.
Stop fucking with me, please, and sleep.

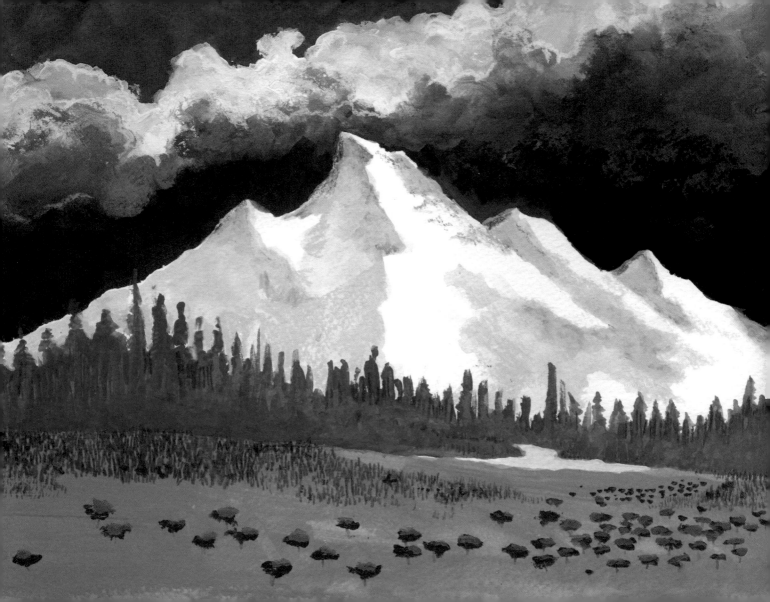

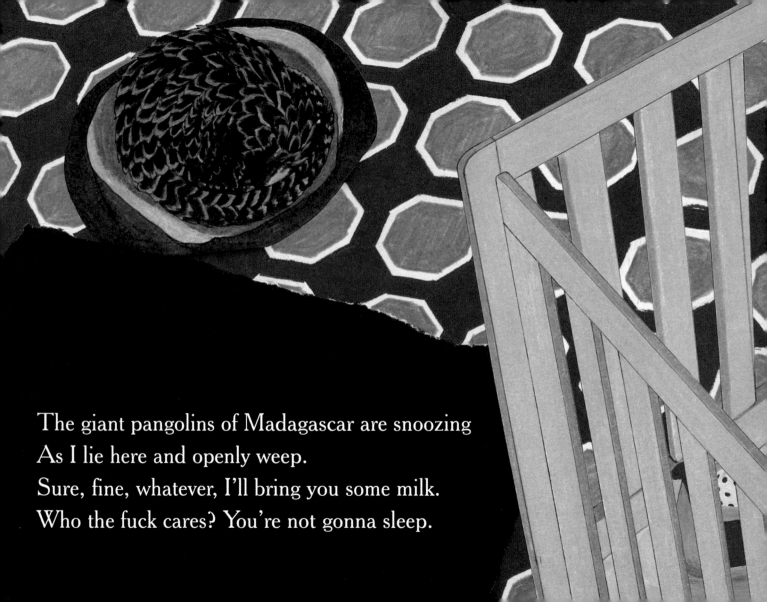

The giant pangolins of Madagascar are snoozing
As I lie here and openly weep.
Sure, fine, whatever, I'll bring you some milk.
Who the fuck cares? You're not gonna sleep.

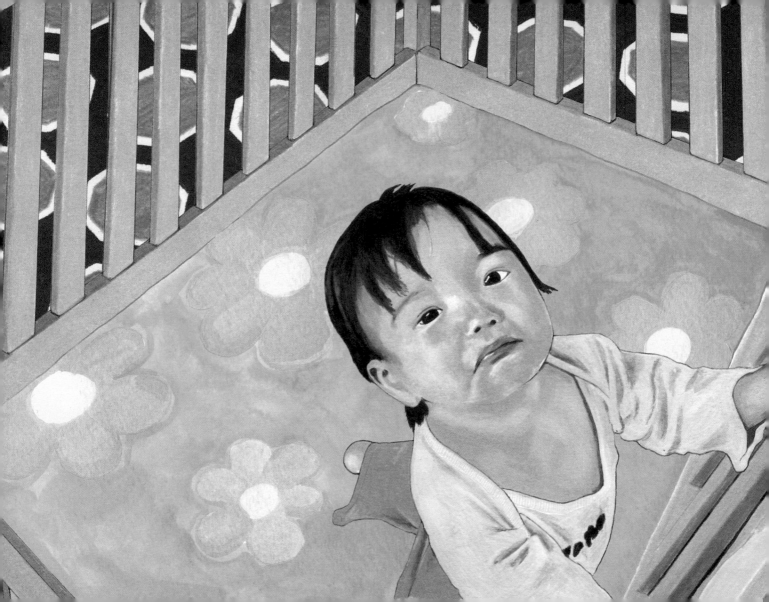

This room is all I can remember,
The furniture crappy and cheap.
You win. You escape. You run down the hall.
As I nod the fuck off, and sleep.

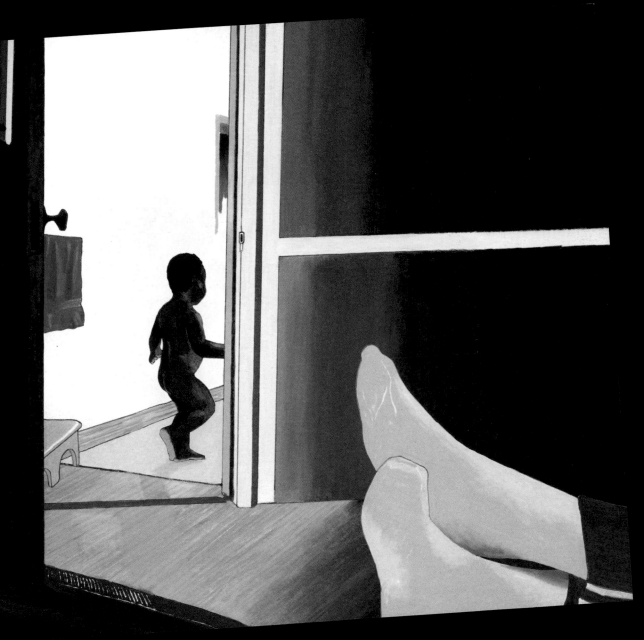

Bleary and dazed I awaken
To find your eyes shut, so I keep
My fingers crossed tight as I tiptoe away
And pray that you're fucking asleep.

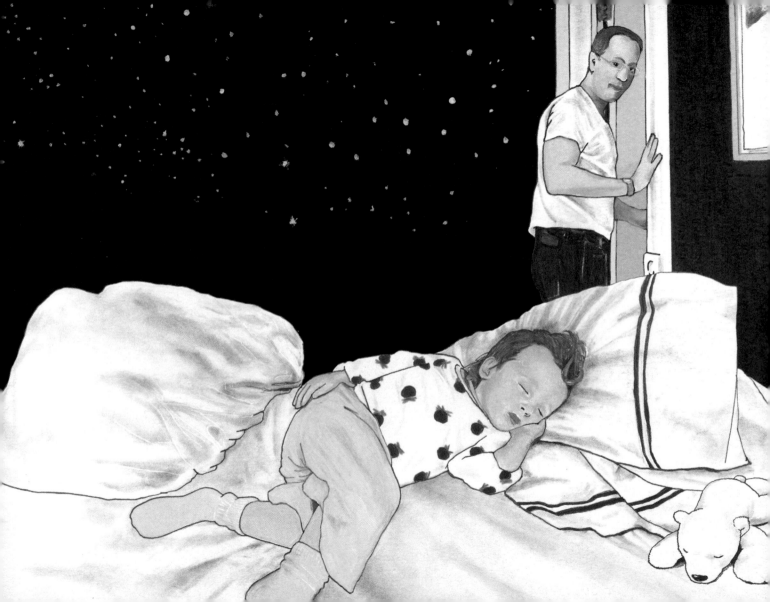

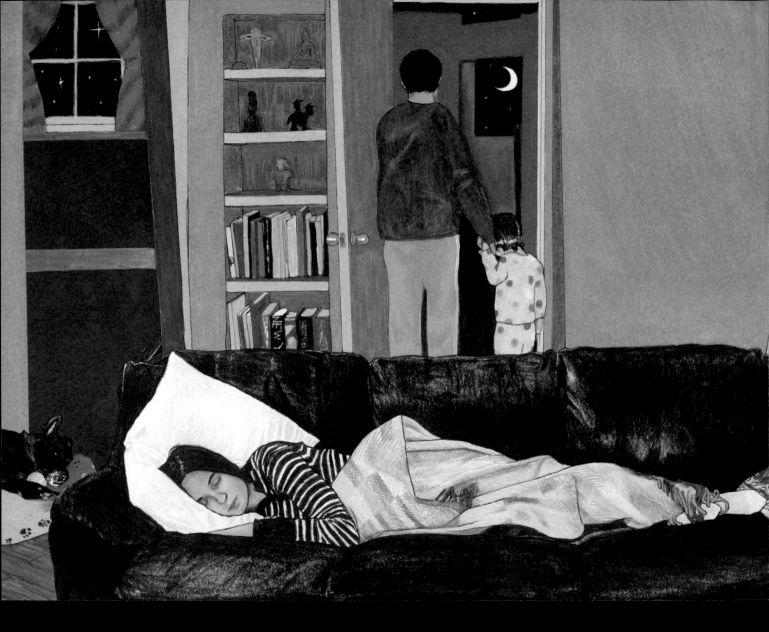

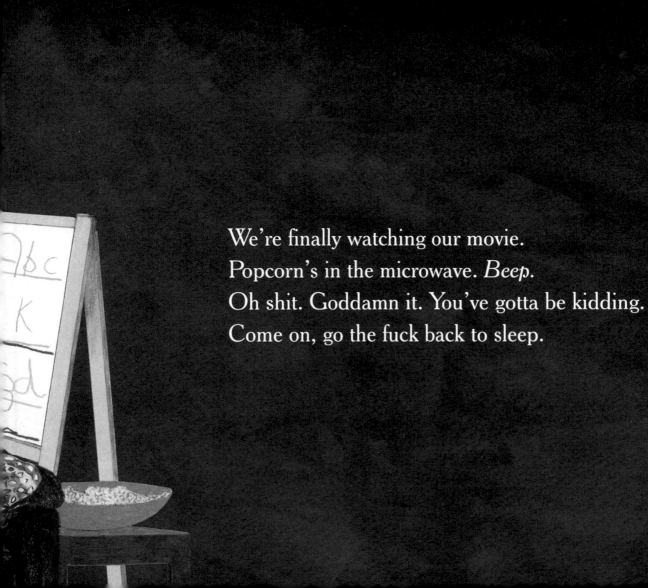

We're finally watching our movie.
Popcorn's in the microwave. *Beep.*
Oh shit. Goddamn it. You've gotta be kidding.
Come on, go the fuck back to sleep.

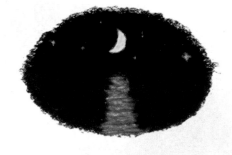

The End